Pretty and Bright

I Talk You Talk Press

Copyright © 2020 I Talk You Talk Press

ISBN: 978-4-909733-41-2

www.italkyoutalk.com

info@italkyoutalk.com

All rights reserved. No part of this publication may be resold, reproduced, stored in retrieval system, copied in any form or by any means, electronic, mechanical, photocopying, recording or otherwise transmitted without the prior written permission from the publisher. You must not circulate this publication in any format, online or otherwise.

This is a work of fiction. Names, characters, businesses, organizations, products, places, events and incidents are either the products of the author's imagination or are used in a fictitious manner. We have no affiliation with any existing companies mentioned in this story. Any resemblance to actual persons, living or dead, existing stories or actual events is purely coincidental.

Although the author and publisher have made every effort to ensure that the contents of this book were correct at press time, the author and publisher do not assume and hereby disclaim any liability to any party for any loss, damage, or disruption caused by errors or omissions, whether such errors or omissions result from negligence, accident, or any other cause.

For more information, see the Copyright Notice on our website.

Image copyright: © Photographee.eu #95823802 Adobe Stock Standard license

CONTENTS

1. Jim Pierce has a new job — 1
2. A man is dead — 3
3. An accident? — 6
4. What did you see? — 10
5. Mrs Frampton — 13
6. The postman — 16
7. Angus — 18
8. Another mystery — 21
9. A big empty house — 26
10. Harriet is very puzzled — 30
11. Walter has an idea — 32
12. Mrs Frampton calls the police station — 37
13. What Mrs Frampton saw — 39

14. Where is Walter?	41
15. Mrs Frampton is worried	43
16. Angus in trouble	44
17. A terrible story	46
18. Eliza	49
19. Through the window	52
20. The next day	55
21. November	57
Thank You	59
About the Author	61

1. JIM PIERCE HAS A NEW JOB

Jim Pierce is the new Police Superintendent in Wolling. He is the boss. He wants to do well in his career. He was very pleased when he got this job.

Jim started working in Wolling on a Monday. At 10:00am he decided to meet his detectives, so he went to the detectives' room. There were four people there. Their names were Mark, Eliza, Keith and Sanjay. They were all young. They were wearing jeans, boots and leather jackets. They looked tough and energetic. Jim liked their style.

"We are looking for drug gangs," they said to Jim.

"I will look at the files for the cases you are working on," he said. "Keep up the good work. But there should be six detectives here. Where is Detective Sergeant Pretty?"

"He didn't come to work today," answered Mark. "He has a bad back. He is going to see the doctor."

"And where is Detective Constable Bright? Is she sick too?"

"We don't know," said Eliza. "She is new. Today is her first day, but we haven't seen her."

Jim thought it was strange. "OK. We will meet again tomorrow morning. I want a report from everyone.

Jim had a good meeting on Tuesday morning with his detectives. Detective Sergeant Pretty was still at home. He was sick. But Detective Constable Bright was there.

"Where were you yesterday?" Jim asked her.

Amelia Bright's face turned red.

"I am very sorry, Sir. I don't know this area well. I am renting a house on a farm out in the country. I left home on my bicycle very early, but I got lost. I went the wrong way. I didn't get to Wolling until 11:30am."

"Your bicycle!" Jim was very surprised. "Why did you ride a bicycle?"

"I don't have a car, Sir. There are no buses from my house to Wolling. And I like to ride my bike. I like to be healthy."

Jim had read Detective Constable Bright's file. He knew that her first name was Amelia. He knew that she was a new graduate from the police college. Wolling was her first job.

He looked at Amelia. She was very tall and thin. Her hair was very blonde. It looked white. She had very big blue eyes. Her face was red, and she had tears in her eyes.

She looks about 16 years old, thought Jim. *Why couldn't I have a tough, strong, young man or woman? I think she is weak.*

2. A MAN IS DEAD

On Wednesday, a postman telephoned the police station.

"I tried to put a letter in the letterbox at two three four Skillington Road," he said. "The letterbox is full. The front door is open. I think something is wrong."

Two policemen went to the house to look. They found an old man on the floor in the living room. His head was covered in blood. He was dead. One of the policemen called the station.

"An old man who lived at two three four Skillington Road is dead. We think it was an accident. We think he fell over. But the front door was open, so we are not sure. Maybe there was a robber. Please send a medical team, the crime scene team and some detectives."

Jim went to the detectives' room. Amelia Bright was there. She was working on a computer. There was a man there, too. He was reading a newspaper.

"Are you Detective Sergeant Pretty?" asked Jim.

The man stood up. "Yes. That's me. Walter Pretty. I guess you are Superintendent Pierce. Nice to meet you, Sir."

He shook hands with Jim.

His hand was soft. He was short and fat. His hair was thin and grey. He was wearing a grey suit and a shirt and tie.

"I'm sorry I wasn't here when you arrived. My back was painful. I went to the doctor. He told me to take another day off work."

Jim wasn't happy. *Detective Sergeant Pretty looks lazy. How can I be successful when I only have four real detectives? Why do I have this young woman who gets lost, and a small, fat man?*

He told Walter and Amelia about the old man in Skillington Road.

"Go there now. It will be easy. The policemen at the house think the old man fell and hit his head. A simple accident."

Amelia and Walter picked up their jackets and walked out.

Jim went back to his office. *I need new detectives,* he thought. *I want two new detectives who are energetic and smart. Why is Walter Pretty still working? Why hasn't he retired?*

Everything in the Wolling Police Station was new to Jim. But he had someone to help him. Mary Jane Williams had been at the police station for a long time. She managed everything - the office, the policemen and the detectives. Today she was working on the front desk because the desk sergeant was not working. She knew everything about the police station, and the people who worked there.

Jim called Mary Jane. "Can you come to my office? I want to talk to you."

"No," she said. "I can't do that. I am on the front desk today. I must stay here."

"OK," said Jim. "I will come and see you."

Mary Jane was very busy. Everyone who came to the police station talked to her. She answered questions. She told people what to do. She gave people forms to fill in. She told people where to go, or where to wait. Finally, she was free to talk to Jim.

"Do you know Walter Pretty?" he asked.

"Yes, of course," said Mary Jane. "He has been here a long time."

"I looked at his records. He is almost sixty. Why is he only a Detective Sergeant?"

"He didn't want to be an Inspector," answered Mary Jane.

Jim didn't understand. "Why not?"

"I don't know. Some people like their jobs. They don't want to change. Maybe Walter is like that."

"Why doesn't he retire?" asked Jim. "I only talked to him for a few minutes, but I know he is fat, lazy and slow. I don't want him. I want good results from this police station."

Mary Jane became angry.

"Walter has been a policeman for more than thirty years. He works very hard. Maybe he is too old-fashioned for you. Maybe the younger detectives laugh at him. But he is a very good detective. I think he is the best detective in Wolling."

"But he's old!" Jim was surprised because Mary Jane was angry.

"He has no children. His wife was the owner of a small hotel. She died. He lives there alone. If he retired, what would he do? Sit in a big empty house and wait to die? He does very good work here."

A woman came into the police station. She walked up to the desk and said, "I have lost my dog."

"I'm busy," said Mary Jane to Jim. "You should look at the records. Walter Pretty has been very successful. You are lucky to have him on your team."

Jim walked away. He didn't say anything, but he thought, *Maybe Walter Pretty is very good at finding lost dogs and stolen TVs. But life is different now. I want detectives who can solve the crimes that get into the newspapers and on the TV. Drugs, murder…*

3. AN ACCIDENT?

Amelia and Walter walked out to the car park.

"We'll take my car," said Walter.

They drove to Skillington Road. It was a long road. On one side, there were small houses, and on the other side there was a river. There was a park and a walkway between the river and the road. The sun was shining. Parents were in the park with babies and children. Everything was very quiet and peaceful.

A police car and the vans for the crime scene team and the medical team were parked outside number 234. Walter parked his car.

They walked through the front door. The house was small. There was a small kitchen and a living room downstairs. The living room was full of people. The medical team and crime scene workers were all busy. Two young policemen were in the kitchen.

"Good morning," said Walter.

"Hi, Walter," said one of the policemen.

Amelia was shocked. *They should call him Sir!* she thought.

Walter didn't seem to mind. "Amelia, this is Joe Begg and Neil Warren. Joe, Neil, this is Detective Constable Bright. Did you talk to the postman?"

"Yes," said Neil. "His name is Frank Eastman. He wanted to go back to work. I wrote everything down. He doesn't know anything. He wanted to put a letter in the letter box. The box was full. He opened it. He saw two newspapers and some letters. Then he saw the open door. So he called the police station."

"What is the dead man's name?" asked Amelia.

"The postman said, 'The name on the letters is Joseph Jones,'" said Joe.

The police doctor came into the kitchen. "Hi Walter," she said. "I have finished. I want to take the body away. Do you want to come and look at him first?"

"Yes, please." Walter went into the living room. Amelia followed him.

The photographer and others were still working. Amelia didn't know what to do, so she watched Walter. He stood next to the body and looked around. He didn't speak or move, but he spent a long time looking. Amelia thought it was very strange. She looked at the police doctor. The police doctor laughed. "I have worked with Walter many times. He always does this. You're new, aren't you?"

"Yes," said Amelia. "I'm Amelia Bright. I started work on Monday."

"I'm Harriet Broadman. Welcome to Wolling. I hope you like it here."

"Harriet?" said Walter. "What happened?"

"I don't know. He has a big cut on his head. It killed him. There is blood on the edge of the table. Maybe he fell and hit his head. I'll tell you more after I have looked at the body in my examination room. But I'm very busy. I'm sorry but I can't give you a report before Friday, or maybe Monday."

"OK, Harriet. I understand. You can take the body away," said Walter.

Harriet's team put the dead man in a body bag and then onto a stretcher. They carried it out of the house.

Walter turned to a man in a white overall. "Brian, what do you know about Mr Jones?"

Brian was watching the photographer take pictures of the room. "Is that his name?"

"The postman said the letter was addressed to Joseph Jones," said Walter.

"We haven't found any bank books or credit cards or letters. We didn't find a passport. There is no telephone. We looked upstairs. We didn't find anything there either."

"OK, Brian. Thank you. Will your people keep looking?"

"Of course, Walter. We will do a good job. I know you will want to look for yourself. But I'm guessing this is an accident."

"Thanks, Brian."

Amelia and Walter went into the garden. Walter walked around the house. He looked at the back windows. He put on gloves and opened the letterbox. There were two newspapers, but no letters. He went back inside the house. "Joe!" he shouted. Joe came out of the kitchen.

"Where did you speak to the postman?" asked Walter.

"The postman was waiting on the road when we arrived. He didn't want to go into the house. We talked to him by the front gate."

"What did he do with the letter?" asked Walter.

Joe was puzzled. "The letter? Oh, I understand. The letter he wanted to put in the letterbox. Sorry. I don't know."

"Did Brian's team look in the letterbox?" asked Walter.

"I don't think so," answered Joe. "I'll tell them you want them to look at it."

"Thank you, Joe," said Walter. "Amelia and I will look around the house. You and Neil can wait outside."

"OK, boss," said Joe.

Walter and Amelia spent more than an hour in the house. First, they went upstairs. There were two bedrooms and a bathroom. Walter stood in the middle of each room and looked around. Amelia opened doors and drawers and looked for hints about the old man's life. There were clothes in the drawers. They were normal clothes and they all came from English department stores. The shoes and coats and jackets in the closets were the same. There was nothing special. Amelia looked at everything in the bathroom. Toothpaste, soap, toilet paper, shaving cream, a razor. She looked in the small cupboard behind the bathroom mirror. She found some pain killers and some cough medicine, but nothing else.

Walter didn't touch anything. He didn't speak. Finally, he said, "Let's see if they have finished downstairs."

Amelia followed Walter downstairs. *What is he doing?* she thought. *Joe and Neil think it was an accident. Mr Jones fell and hit his head. Brian and Harriet, the police doctor, think so too. Why are we still here?*

Downstairs, the workers had gone. Walter looked at the books in the living room. They were detective stories and thrillers.

They looked in the kitchen. The old man had cans of soup, a few vegetables, some sausages and eggs in the refrigerator.

Finally, Walter spoke again. "Let's go to a café and have a cup of tea," he said.

4. WHAT DID YOU SEE?

Walter and Amelia went to a café near the police station. It was very busy. The customers were mostly shoppers.

"What do you want?" asked Walter. "Tea? Coffee?"

"I'll have tea, please," said Amelia. "Milk. No sugar." She sat down at a table. Walter went to the counter and came back with two cups of tea.

He gave one to Amelia, and sat down on the other side of the table. He drank his tea. Then he said, "What do you think?"

"What do I think?" Amelia didn't understand.

"Was it an accident? Or did Mr Jones find a robber in his house? Was it murder?"

"But they said it was an accident!" Amelia was very puzzled.

"Harriet said 'maybe it was an accident'. And Brian said he was guessing. You must learn to listen very carefully."

"Oh, OK. But we should wait for Harriet's report. She said Friday, or maybe Monday," said Amelia.

"No," said Walter. "If it wasn't an accident, we must start working now. The first twenty-four hours after a murder are very important."

"Murder!" Amelia was amazed. "Why are you thinking about murder?"

Walter laughed. "I don't know if Mr Jones was murdered. Maybe it was an accident. Maybe it was a robbery. But we saw some strange things."

"We did?" Amelia drank her tea very fast. Walter told her to look and listen. She listened, and she looked, but she didn't think anything was strange.

"Think, Amelia. Think!" said Walter.

Then Amelia remembered. "The postman said there were some letters and two newspapers in the letterbox. But when you looked, there were no letters!"

"Yes," said Walter. "And what about the letter the postman wanted to deliver today? Where is it? And there's something else."

Amelia was excited. "The front door wasn't locked! Maybe Mr Jones had a visitor?"

So what do you think we should do?" asked Walter.

Amelia thought hard. "We should talk to the postman. Maybe he took the letters away. And we must talk to the neighbours. Maybe they saw or heard something."

"Good!" said Walter. "We will go back to the police station and make a report. We will tell Superintendent Pierce that we have things to check. There are some questions without answers."

Back at the police station, Amelia and Walter talked to Jim Pierce. He was angry. "It is easy. The old man fell over and hit his head. It was an accident!"

"Maybe," said Walter. "When we get a report from Harriet, the police doctor, we will know more. But we must wait until Friday or Monday for her report. I want to check up on the letters, and talk to the neighbours now."

These detectives are no good, thought Jim. *I can't use them for real police work. This will keep them busy and out of the office.*

"OK," he said. "You can spend the rest of today, and some time tomorrow checking. But I think it is a waste of time. You won't find anything. It was an accident."

Walter and Amelia went back to the detectives' room.

"Please find out as much as you can about Joseph Jones," said Walter. "There were no photographs or letters. We didn't find a bankbook or a library card or a passport. Don't you think it is strange? Then please write up a report about everything we know."

Amelia sat down at her computer and started searching for information about Joseph Jones. She couldn't find a bank account. The electricity company said he paid his bills in cash. The house rental company said the same thing. Then she wrote the report. It was the first time she had written a report, and she wanted to make a good job. When she finished, she looked at the time on her computer screen. It was 6:30pm.

The four young detectives were at their desks. They were talking and laughing loudly. They were going to a bar for drinks after work. They didn't ask Amelia to join them. She felt sad and lonely. *I have to cycle fourteen kilometres to my house in the country,* she thought. *It was sunny today, but now it's dark and cold. I must leave as soon as I can.*

Walter came back to the office. He nodded to Amelia and sat down at his desk. She looked across at Walter. He was looking up at the ceiling.

Maybe he is thinking. He is a little strange, and it seems the other detectives don't like him.

Amelia shut down her computer. She took her jacket and bag and walked out.

"Good night, Walter!" she called. But Walter didn't answer. Amelia went to the locker room and changed into her cycling clothes.

She was very cold when she arrived at the little house in the country.

I'll have a hot bath, she thought. *Then I'll feel warmer.*

She went to the tiny bathroom at the back of the house. She turned on the hot water tap – nothing! She went to the kitchen and tried the hot tap there. Some brown water came out, then there was nothing.

I have no hot water!

Amelia called the farmer who owned the house. "I have no hot water," she said.

"Oh. No problem. I will come one day next week and fix it," said the farmer cheerfully.

Next week! thought Amelia. *That's terrible!* But she didn't say anything. The house was very, very cheap. She had very little money, and she knew she couldn't pay for anything better.

Amelia didn't want anyone to know that she had very little money. Her sister had no husband, and three small children. Her sister had money problems. Amelia sent her money. So she had no money for a car, or a nice apartment in the city with hot water.

5. MRS FRAMPTON

Amelia came into work on Thursday morning. She went to the locker room and changed into her work clothes. When Amelia went into the detectives' room, the other detectives didn't say 'hello' or 'good morning'. They were talking about Walter.

"Silly old fool," said Mark. "He can't work on a real murder. So he pretends that the accident in the house on Skillington Road was a murder!"

"The Superintendent is very angry. He wants Walter to retire," said Sanjay.

"But where would Walter go? To a farm for old donkeys?" laughed Mark.

Amelia felt bad. Walter was very kind to her yesterday. She thought he was a nice man. His way of working was a little strange, but Amelia thought he knew a lot about being a detective.

She heard a small cough. She looked up. Walter was standing by the door. *Oh no!* thought Amelia. *Walter heard what Mark said.*

But Walter didn't look unhappy or angry. He smiled and said, "Come on, Amelia, we have work to do."

They walked out to Walter's car. "Why don't you talk to the postman?" said Walter. "I will drive you to the post office. When you finish, you can meet me in Skillington Road. I will talk to the neighbours."

"But…," Amelia felt nervous. "What will I ask the postman?"

Walter laughed. "Amelia! The letters! Did he take the letters out of the letterbox? What did he do with the letter he brought yesterday?"

"OK. I can do that," said Amelia.

"Of course you can," said Walter, smiling.

When Walter arrived in Skillington Road, he knocked on the door of number 232. There was no answer. He went to number 236. He rang the doorbell.

He heard a woman's voice call out. "Come in! The door's unlocked!"

He opened the door and walked in. "In here!" The voice came from the living room at the front of the house.

Walter walked into the living room. A very old lady was sitting in a wheelchair by the window. She had a lot of white hair, and very bright brown eyes.

"Are you a policeman?" she asked.

"Yes," answered Walter. I am Detective Sergeant Walter Pretty from Wolling Police Station. May I have your name?"

"I'm Gert Frampton. Please sit down." Mrs Frampton pointed to an armchair.

Walter sat down. "Mrs Frampton! It is very dangerous for you to have your front door unlocked! Someone might come in and attack you."

Mrs Frampton laughed. "I see everyone who walks up to my front door. I have an emergency alarm and a telephone. I'm always safe. I see everything that happens on this part of Skillington Road. I saw you with the policemen yesterday. So I know you are not here to hurt me."

This is lucky, thought Walter. *I am sure Mrs Frampton can give me some useful information.*

"Yesterday, the postman called us. There were two newspapers in your next-door neighbour's letterbox. The front door was open, and the postman was worried. When the policemen went into the house, they found Mr Jones dead. Probably, it was an accident. But we have to check everything. Did you know Mr Jones?"

"I didn't know his name. Jones? He always looked foreign to me."

Walter smiled. He looked at Mrs Frampton. *Her eyes are bright, she is thinking hard. Mrs Frampton is smart,* thought Walter. *She sees things.*

Mrs Frampton said, "He came to this road about five years ago. I never talked to him. I never go out, but I saw him many times. He went out every Monday and Thursday. He came back with supermarket bags."

"Did he often have visitors?"

"I never saw any visitors," answered Mrs Frampton. "Maybe he had visitors at night. I close the curtains, and watch TV from seven pm. I don't see or hear anything at night."

"Did you hear any noise from Mr Jones' house on Monday night or Tuesday?"

"No," said Mrs Frampton.

"Did you see anything strange this week? Was anything different?" asked Walter.

"There was something different," said Mrs Frampton. "But maybe it has nothing to do with Mr Jones."

"What was it?" asked Walter.

"Look out of the window," said Mrs Frampton. "Do you see the bus stop across the road?"

Walter looked out the window. There was a bus stop opposite Mr Jones' house. It had a shelter and a seat. "Yes, I see it," said Walter.

"About a year ago, an old man started sitting on that seat every day. He never gets on a bus. He sits and looks across the road at these houses. He wears a hat and scarf and a long coat. I saw him on Monday and Tuesday. But I didn't see him yesterday. He is not there today. That is different."

"That is interesting. Do you know anything else about this man?"

"No. But I think maybe he is homeless. He wears the same clothes in winter and summer. He looks poor. He comes to the bus stop from down by the river. I read there are homeless people living under the bridges. Maybe he is one of them."

Walter thanked Mrs Frampton. He asked her to be careful about her unlocked door. He went out of the house and walked across the road.

Maybe the old man who sits at the bus stop saw something, he thought. *I must find him.*

6. THE POSTMAN

Amelia went into the post office. She went to the mailroom and asked to speak to Frank Eastman. "He's not here right now," said the manager of the mailroom. "He is delivering some parcels. Can you wait? He will be back soon."

Amelia waited. She had to wait for an hour, but finally, Frank came back.

"Frank," said Amelia. "Yesterday, when you tried to deliver the letter, you saw two newspapers and some other letters in the mailbox. Is that right?"

"Yes," said Frank. "I tried to put the letter in the box, but it was full. I thought it was strange, so I opened the box. There were three letters and two newspapers. I pushed yesterday's letter in on top and closed the box."

"So there should be four letters in the letter box?"

"Yes," answered Frank.

"But when we looked in the letter box, there were no letters," Amelia told Frank. "Where are the letters?"

Frank looked worried. "I don't know. I put one envelope in, but I didn't take anything out!"

"Did you notice anything about the letters?" asked Amelia.

"I don't think so," said Frank.

"Please think hard, Frank. Anything will help. Were they bills? Post cards? Private letters?"

"There was a bill, maybe from the electricity company, and something that looked like advertising. I didn't see the other letter. It was at the bottom of the box."

"And yesterday's letter?" asked Amelia.

"Oh, I saw that one, of course. I was looking at it, and wondering what to do."

"And?" asked Amelia.

"The envelope was hand-written. It was from another country."

"Was the envelope a normal size?" Amelia wanted as much information as possible.

"Yes. It was normal. There was nothing special about it."

"But Frank." Amelia was puzzled. "You waited for the policemen outside the house. How could the letters and newspapers have disappeared?"

"Well, I went to telephone the police. I have my mobile phone. But this was work. I came back here, and called them. My boss said to go back and wait for the police. So I went back."

"How long were you away?" asked Amelia.

"Maybe twenty or twenty-five minutes."

Amelia thanked Frank and left the post office. She walked to 234 Skillington Road. There was a policeman standing outside.

"Have you seen Walter?" she asked.

"Yes. He came out of the house next-door, number two three six. He walked across the road towards the river."

"When was that?"

"About forty minutes ago."

"I want to go into Mr Jones' house again," said Amelia. "Do you have the keys?"

"Sure," said the policeman. He unlocked the door.

Amelia took some gloves from her bag and put them on as she went into the house.

I didn't see any letters here yesterday, but maybe someone put the missing letters in the house. She searched everywhere but she didn't find the letters. She sat down on the sofa to wait for Walter.

7. ANGUS

Walter walked down to the river. He looked to the right and to the left. There were two bridges. He saw someone sitting under the bridge to the right, so he walked that way. As he got closer, he saw a homeless people's camp between the river and the road. He walked slowly towards it. It was very clean and tidy. Walter was surprised. Often homeless people's camps are very untidy and dirty. This one was different. A row of shopping carts was lined up on one side. Each cart had plastic bags inside. Walter guessed the bags were filled with clothes and blankets and sleeping bags. There was an old picnic table with garden chairs around it. Under the table were plastic laundry baskets with pots, glasses and plates. A young boy was sitting at the table reading a book. He heard Walter's footsteps and turned around. He stood up.

"What do you want?" he asked.

"I am looking for an old man who sits in the bus stop every day. Someone told me he might live here."

"There's no old man here," said the boy.

"I can see that," said Walter looking around. "Where is everyone?"

"Out," said the boy.

"Out where?" asked Walter.

"Why do you want to know?"

"I hope someone can tell me about the old man. I want to talk to him."

"Why do you want to talk to him?"

"Can I sit down?" asked Walter.

"OK." The boy looked angry, but he pointed to a chair, and Walter sat down. The boy looked at Walter.

"What's your name?" asked Walter.

"Angus."

"OK, Angus. I will explain. On Monday night or Tuesday, an old man died in the house across the road from the bus stop. Some people think it was an accident. He fell and hit his head. I am not sure. I think maybe there was a robbery. Maybe he was murdered. The man in the bus stop might have seen something. That's why I want to talk to him."

"You're a policeman?"

"Yes. I'm Detective Sergeant Walter Pretty."

"Police!" shouted Angus. "You are all the same! There is a crime in the area, and you think a homeless person did it!"

"I didn't say that," said Walter quietly.

"No! But that's what you think, isn't it?"

"No. It's not. Maybe it was an accident. I don't know, but I have to ask questions. Do you know the old man who sits in the bus stop?"

"Yes, I do. But he won't talk to you."

"Why not?" asked Walter.

"He doesn't like people. That's why he doesn't live here with us. He hates to talk to people, and he hates to have people near him."

"So how do you know him?" asked Walter.

"One night I found him lying near the river. He was very drunk. I look after him. I take food and leave it near where he sleeps. He talks to me a little. I don't know why. I help him when I can."

"Can you show me where he sleeps?"

"I don't want to do that," answered Angus.

"Please, Angus. I promise I won't talk to him if he doesn't want to speak. Maybe you can ask some questions for me."

"OK." Angus didn't look happy. He picked up his book from the table and put it in a supermarket bag. He put the bag in one of the supermarket trolleys.

Walter was interested in the book. *Angus is reading a book about law. Why is he doing that?*

"Come with me," said Angus. He started walking very quickly along the riverbank.

"Why are you reading a book about law?" Walter asked Angus.

"Why not? Do you think a homeless kid can't read?"

"No. I am sure you can read. But reading a book about law is unusual."

"I want to know about the law. I want to help the other people who live here."

"Why don't you go to a school or college to study?" Walter thought that Angus was a very interesting person.

Angus stopped walking and turned to face Walter. "I didn't finish high school. I have no address and no money. I have been living under the bridge for two years. How can I study at a school?"

Walter felt bad. "Sorry, Angus. I didn't understand."

They walk in silence for a while. "Uh, Angus. How old are you?" asked Walter.

"Sixteen," answered Angus.

"Oh." Walter was shocked. *He is a very handsome young man, he thought. I think he is smart. He cares about other people. He has been homeless since he was fourteen. How did this happen? What is wrong with the world?*

8. ANOTHER MYSTERY

Walter followed Angus to the next bridge.
"He lives here," said Angus.
"What's his name?"
"I don't know. We call him Hatman."
"How often do you come here to see him?"
"Most days. We cook a good meal at night. Everyone eats together. Then I bring some food to him. Sometimes he is not here. Sometimes he is sleeping. He doesn't like me to come close, so I leave the food next to that tree." Angus pointed to a willow tree near the bridge. He walked up to the tree and looked. "That's strange," he said. "The food is still here from yesterday."

Walter walked to the tree and stared at the box. "Can I open it?" he asked Angus.

"Sure."

Walter opened the box. He was surprised. There were two sandwiches, some canned peaches, a piece of steak cut into small pieces and soft potato.

"Do you make this for him every day?" he asked Angus.

"Something like this. The sandwiches are for his breakfast. I cut the meat up small because Hatman's teeth are no good."

"Where does the food come from? Do you buy it?"

Angus laughs. "What with? We have no money! No. We go to restaurants and hotels. They throw a lot of food away. We take the food from their garbage containers. Some of the kitchen people know me. They save leftover food and give it to me."

"I understand. And usually the old man you call Hatman takes the food?" asked Walter.

"Yes. Always," said Angus. "I don't know why he didn't take it last night."

"What time did you bring it?"

"About ten thirty pm. It was dark. I didn't see or hear him. I guessed he was not there, or maybe sleeping."

"I don't want to frighten him. Will you go and see if he is there?" Walter asked Angus.

"OK. You stay here," said Angus.

Walter waited next to the tree and watched Angus walk down the riverbank to the bridge. Angus disappeared under the bridge. Very soon he came out again. He ran towards Walter. "You should come and look!" he shouted.

Walter hurried towards the bridge.

Angus pointed to a pile of clothes and blankets under the bridge. "He's not here. But something is wrong."

Walter didn't understand. "What's wrong?"

"Two things," said Angus. "Hatman never takes his hat or coat off, unless he is sleeping. But they are here. And look at the empty bottle! That's whisky!"

"But you told me you found Hatman drunk. So I guess he drinks whisky."

Walter looked at the whisky bottle. It was an expensive brand. "Maybe someone gave it to him?"

"Who? Why?" asked Angus. Walter could see that Angus was very worried.

"Will you come and have a cup of coffee with me?" he asked Angus. "We can talk about what has happened to Hatman. Maybe you can help me to decide what to do next."

Angus and Walter walked up to the road. "Where's a good café?" asked Walter.

"There's a nice one near the other bridge," said Angus.

Walter and Angus walked along the road. When they walked past Joseph Jones' house, Amelia saw them through the window. She hurried out to meet them, but Walter shook his head. *I don't think Angus will talk to me if Amelia is there,* he thought. Amelia understood Walter's signal and went back into the house.

The café was very nice. Walter and Angus sat down at a table near the window. A waitress came to take their order. Angus asked for a vanilla milkshake. Walter ordered tea. "Do you want anything to eat?" the waitress asked Angus."

"No, thank you," answered Angus. The waitress smiled and went away.

Angus laughed. "The women who own this café are very nice. They leave a bag of leftovers for me every day. I collect the bag from behind the café. They are surprised to see me here as a customer!"

They didn't talk while they waited for their drinks to come.

When the waitress brought their drinks, there was a slice of chocolate cake for Angus. "We know you like it!" said the waitress, smiling.

Walter drank his tea and watched Angus eating the cake. *Everyone likes him. He is a special young person. What happened? Why is he homeless? But I can't ask about that now. I have to find out about the man they call Hatman.*

"Angus. Maybe I have two mysteries now. I don't know. I want to ask Hatman if he saw anything the day Joseph Jones died. I want to find out if Joseph Jones was attacked, or if he had an accident. Now it seems that Hatman is missing. You like the law, so I guess you like facts. What facts do we have?"

Angus stopped eating. He was quiet while he thought. Then he held up his hand and pointed to his fingers as he talked.

"One. Hatman came to live on the riverbank about a year ago. Two. He doesn't like to talk to people. He doesn't like people to be near him. So he lives alone. Three. He has a problem with alcohol. The night I found him drunk, he had found some money in the street. He bought vodka. But usually he has no money to buy vodka or whisky, or anything else. There was an empty whisky bottle next to his blankets."

"It was an expensive bottle of whisky," said Walter.

"That's strange," said Angus. "But let me continue. Four. Hatman always wears his hat and coat. The only time he takes them off is when he is sleeping. He is not at his camp. But his hat and coat are there. Five. The last time I saw him was on Tuesday night. He was lying in his blankets. He waved to me. I left the food and went away. Tuesday's food is gone. Six. I took food to him last night. I didn't see him. Last night's food is still there. This is very strange."

Angus drank some of his milkshake. Then he put down the glass and stared at Walter. "I think there is a mystery."

"I agree," said Walter. "A woman who lives in this street told me that he sat in the bus stop every day. She said he was not there yesterday, and he is not there today. Where has he gone? I want to check all the hospitals. Maybe he became ill or had an accident."

"OK," said Angus. "It is a good idea. Will you come and tell me what you find out?"

"Of course," said Walter.

Angus stood up. "I have to go now. Thank you for the milkshake." He walked quickly out the door.

Walter went to the counter to pay. He wanted to pay for the chocolate cake. "Oh, no!" said the woman at the counter. "That was a present for Angus. He is such a nice boy!"

"He seems very busy," said Walter. "What does he do?"

"He looks after that group of homeless teenagers - the ones that live under the bridge. He's homeless too, but he seems to be a good organiser. And he reads a lot. He can't have a library card because he has no address. He tells me what books he wants, and I take them out of the library for him."

"Do you know the old man who sits in the bus shelter every day?"

"I see him, but I don't know him. He doesn't talk to anyone. People who catch the bus are a little scared of him. No one sits in the bus shelter when he is there, even if it's raining!"

Walter stood on the street outside the café. He called the police station. He asked for someone to call all the hospitals. He said, "Please check if they have a new patient who is an old homeless man."

Then he walked down to Joseph Jones' house to find Amelia.

Amelia said, "Someone took the letters out of the letterbox when Frank went to call the police."

"That's interesting," said Walter. "Come with me and talk to Mrs Frampton. Maybe she saw someone take the letters from the letterbox."

They went to Mrs Frampton's house. "I can see people walk up the path to the front door, but I can't see the letterbox from my window," she said. "I'm sorry but I can't help."

"Are you OK?" Amelia was worried about Mrs Frampton. She was in a wheelchair, and she lived alone.

"Of course I am! I have caregivers who come every day. I have been in a wheelchair for thirteen years. Worry about yourself! You are too thin and pale!"

Amelia laughed. "OK. I'm sorry. Of course, you can look after yourself."

Walter gave Mrs Frampton his business card. "If you think of anything else, will you call me please?"

9. A BIG EMPTY HOUSE

Back at the police station, Walter disappeared, and Amelia went to the detective's room. She sat down at her desk and started to write a report. Eliza came in.

"Why are you working?" she asked Amelia. "It's time to go home."

Amelia turned and smiled at Eliza. Amelia was wearing a black pants suit and a white shirt. Eliza thought she looked old-fashioned. Eliza was wearing jeans, boots and red leather jacket. *Does she think she's a secretary?* Eliza asked herself. *Doesn't she know what a real detective looks like?*

"I must write this report," said Amelia. "Then I'll go home."

Eliza was going out drinking with the other detectives. She felt bad because Amelia was alone. *I could ask her to join us in the bar,* she thought. *But the guys would laugh at me.*

"OK. See you tomorrow," she said. She picked up her bag and went out.

About half an hour later, Mary Jane walked past the detectives' room and looked through the door. She saw Amelia sitting at her desk, typing on her computer. She looked very lonely. Mary Jane went into the room.

"Did you have a good day?" she asked Amelia.

Amelia turned and looked at Mary Jane. Amelia's eyes filled with tears.

"What's wrong?" asked Mary Jane.

"Superintendent Pierce sent me out with Walter. I know Walter is very kind. But the other detectives laugh at him. They are laughing at me. I don't belong here!"

Mary Jane was angry. She sat down next to Amelia. "Listen to me, you silly girl!" she said.

Amelia looked at Mary Jane. Mary Jane was about 50 years old. She looked strong and tough. Amelia knew that Mary Jane was angry, but she didn't know why.

"Superintendent Jim Pierce has a new job. It's a big promotion for him. He dreams about being on the TV news, and in the newspapers. He wants to be the big crime-fighting boss. He wants to be famous.

"Mark, Eliza, Keith and Sanjay look like detectives from a TV drama series. Jim Pierce thinks they are great detectives.

"All the uniformed policemen here want to be like them. They think they are cool. But if you ask them who they want to work with, their answer is different. Walter knows their names. He is always polite to them. He doesn't make mistakes. You are lucky. You want to learn to be a detective? Stay with Walter!"

Mary Jane stood up and walked out of the office. Amelia looked at her computer screen. Her report was almost finished.

It's late and I'm tired. Maybe I can come in early tomorrow and finish it.

Amelia went to the locker room and changed into her cycling clothes. She went out to the car park. It was dark and raining heavily. *Oh no!* thought Amelia. *I'll get wet and cold and there's no hot water at my house.*

She walked to her bicycle, and unlocked the chain. Someone came up next to her. Amelia jumped.

It was Walter. "What are you doing?" he asked.

"I'm going home. I'll finish the report in the morning."

"Where do you live?"

"I rent a house out in the country."

"But you can't cycle there in this weather!" Walter was shocked. "Come and stay at my house."

"Uh, thank you. But I'll be OK," she said.

"I have eight spare bedrooms and three bathrooms. You can have the second floor of my house all to yourself."

Amelia looked at the rain. She thought about the long bike ride. She remembered there was no hot water in her house.

"Thank you, Walter. I would like to stay at your house, if it is not too much trouble."

Amelia went back to the locker room and collected her work clothes. Walter drove her to his house. It was very large. It had three floors. There were no lights on. He drove around the back of the house to an empty car park. Walter parked the car, and hurried through the rain to a door at the back of the house. He unlocked the door and turned on the lights. Amelia followed Walter through the door.

They were standing in a large kitchen. It didn't look like anyone used it.

"Do you live here alone?" asked Amelia

"Yes. There is a small apartment here on the ground floor. I live there. The rest of the house is empty. I'll turn on the water heater for the second-floor bathroom, and we'll find some sheets and towels."

Amelia followed Walter up the stairs. He turned the lights on. On the second floor, Amelia saw a hallway with doors. Most doors had numbers on them. "Oh, it was a hotel!" she said.

"Yes. It belonged to my wife's family. She ran the hotel until she died. Now there is only me living here."

"Oh, I'm sorry." Amelia thought it was sad. Walter walked to the end of the hallway and took sheets and towels from a large closet. "These have not been used for more than two years, I hope they are OK. The bathroom is here."

He went into the bathroom and soon came out again. "I have turned on the water heater. In maybe an hour, the water will be hot. Why don't you sleep in the bedroom next to the bathroom? I'll go downstairs and make a cup of tea. Come down when you're ready."

Amelia made the bed in the big old-fashioned bedroom, and turned on the room heater. It was still raining, and the room felt cold.

She found Walter in a small kitchen next to the big hotel kitchen. He had made tea. He pointed to the teapot. "Help yourself."

Amelia poured a cup of tea and sat down. She looked around the room. There was an old sofa against one wall, and an armchair facing a small television. *Walter must spend most of his time here,* she thought.

Amelia enjoyed the evening very much. Walter ordered Chinese food. They talked about Joseph Jones and the Hatman. Amelia realised she had been lonely. Walter didn't ask her any questions about herself, but Amelia told him about her sister and the three children. "I try to help her as much as I can. I send money every month. I am living as cheaply as possible. That's why I don't have a car. That's why I am living out in the country."

"I think that's a bad idea," says Walter. "We often have to work late, or start work early. And it's not safe for you to ride so far alone. When you have been here longer, the local criminals will know who you are. You could be attacked sometime."

Amelia sighed. "I know. I have to find a one-room apartment in town. It was a silly idea to rent that house on the farm."

10. HARRIET IS VERY PUZZLED

Amelia slept well. When she woke up, she took a long shower, got dressed and went downstairs. She felt good. Walter was sitting at the kitchen table reading the newspaper. "Good morning Amelia," he said cheerfully. "Did you sleep well?"

"Very well, thank you. The bed was very comfortable."

"There's bread for toast there, and a fresh pot of tea," Walter pointed to the table. He started reading his newspaper again.

Walter's mobile rang. "Harriet! You're at work very early! Oh, I see. Yes, I know you're very busy but it's terrible that you are starting work at six o'clock..... What? OK, Amelia and I will be there very soon."

"That was Harriet, the police doctor. She says maybe she is going crazy. She wants us to go to her office as soon as possible. Hurry up with your breakfast. I'll finish getting ready for work."

Amelia jumped up and went upstairs, eating her toast as she climbed. *I have to tidy the bedroom and take the sheets off. I have to pack my bag,* she thought.

She heard Walter shouting from the bottom of the stairs. "Leave everything. We can come back later."

"OK." Amelia grabbed her shoulder bag and ran downstairs.

Harriet Broadman was waiting for them in her examination room. "You were quick!" she said. "Come and look at this."

There were two bodies lying on tables in the centre of the room. They were covered with sheets.

"Late Tuesday night, someone saw a man's body in the river. It was brought here. Another job for me! I came in early, because I am very busy. I thought I could do the check on the man from Skillington Road today. But then I thought, The body from the river. It came in earlier. He probably drowned. It will be quick to find out. So I decided to start with him. My assistants got the body out of cold storage and put it on the table. I took the sheet off and I said, 'You've made a mistake! This is the man from Skillington Road. Get me the body from the river.' They said, 'We didn't make a mistake.' But they went and got the body from the drawer labelled 'Joseph Jones, Skillington Road'.

"They put it on the other table. I took the sheet off and I thought I was going crazy! See what you think."

Harriet took both sheets off. Amelia, Walter and Harriet stared at the two bodies.

"Do you see what I see?" Harriet asked.

Walter leant over one body, and then the other. "Interesting! Which one is Joseph Jones?"

Harriet pointed to the one on the table nearer the door. "That one. He has a big cut on the back of his head. The other one doesn't. I will check the drowned man first. Then I'll check Joseph Jones. But this is the first time for me to check two men who look like twins!"

"Will you be able to find out from DNA?" asked Amelia.

"Of course," said Harriet. "I'll try to send you the results of my first examinations late today. The full report with the chemical tests and DNA will be ready late Monday."

11. WALTER HAS AN IDEA

When they arrived at the police station, Walter said, "You have a report to finish. Why don't you do that? I am going to think."

He walked away and Amelia went to the detectives' room. She passed Mary Jane. Mary Jane was shouting at Sanjav. "I don't care who you think you are! Do not park in the visitors' car park!"

Sanjay smiled at her and walked away. Mary Jane turned to Amelia. "He does it every day. His car park is about fifteen metres further away. He thinks he's such an important person."

"Um, Mary Jane?" Amelia wanted to ask Mary Jane a question, but she was not sure she should ask.

"Yes?" Mary Jane smiled at her, and Amelia felt more confident.

"Walter said he was going to think, and then he disappeared. Where did he go?"

Mary Jane laughed. "There is an old storeroom where we keep the old paper files and evidence boxes. Of course, everything is on computers now, but Walter goes and sits in the storeroom. Don't ask me why. But it seems to work."

Amelia finished her report. Then she had an idea. She called Harriet. One of her assistants answered the phone. "Harriet is busy," he said. "Can I help?"

"Can you send me photographs of the two dead men?" asked Amelia.

"But you should have them by now," answered the assistant. "Walter called about ten minutes ago and asked for them."

Walter came into the detectives' room. "I have a lot of thinking to do but it will have to wait." He opened an email. "Can you print these photographs for me?" he asked Amelia.

Amelia printed the photographs, and looked at them. The two old men looked very similar. She gave them to Walter. "I am going to talk to some people by the river," he said.

"Can I come?" asked Amelia.

"I don't think that's a good idea," answered Walter. Amelia looked disappointed and Walter felt bad.

"OK, come with me. But you might have to stay in the car. I don't know who will be by the river."

In the car, Amelia felt angry. *Walter has ideas and plans but he doesn't tell me anything!*

"Walter. Please tell me. Who are you going to talk to? And why is it important?"

Walter looked at Amelia. "Sorry. We are partners on this case. It is a long time since I had a partner. I forgot. I should tell you everything.

"There is a group of young homeless people living down by the river. I only met one of them. His name is Angus. I think he is an amazing young man. He seems to be their leader. He also looks after an old man who lives alone. The old man has disappeared. I think he is the old man who was found in the river. Homeless people don't like the police. I am worried that if you come with me, Angus will not talk."

"OK, I understand," said Amelia.

"I want to say something else." Walter was not sure how to say it.

"Yes?"

"Your clothes. Your black suit and white shirt. You look like an office worker or a government worker. It will make them nervous. Do you think you could wear more casual clothes?"

Amelia was embarrassed. "I don't have clothes like Eliza! I thought I should look professional. I bought this suit to wear to work."

Walter is wearing an old suit and old shoes. Why is he being rude about my clothes?

"Yes, you look professional. But professional is scary for homeless people. You don't need to dress like Eliza. But do you have jeans and a sweater? Running shoes?"

"Yes. I have clothes like that." Amelia was still upset. "But they are at the house I rent in the country."

"Don't worry. Forget I said anything," said Walter as he parked the car opposite Joseph Jones' house and got out.

Amelia waited in the car.

Walter soon came back. "I can't see Angus," he said. "But there is a young woman there. She doesn't want to talk to me. Maybe she will talk to you."

Amelia took her suit jacket off. She rolled up the sleeves of her shirt and untied her hair. "OK," she said. "I will try."

Walter showed Amelia the area where the young homeless people lived. "I am going to look for Angus," he said. He walked away.

Amelia walked slowly towards the camp. There was a young woman sitting on the ground. The day was not cold, but she was wrapped in a blanket. The young woman was very pale. She had short purple hair. Amelia came close to her, and then sat on the ground. "Hello," she said quietly. Then she waited.

After a while, the young woman looked at her, and then looked away.

"I am Amelia. Who are you?"

"Cassie."

"Hi, Cassie. Do you want to talk?"

"No."

Amelia waited.

"What do you want?" asked Cassie.

"I am worried about the old man who lived alone at the side of the river near here. I think he had an accident. Have you seen him?"

"No."

Oh, dear, thought Amelia. *This will be difficult.*

"The man who was here before. His name is Walter."

"I know. He said." Cassie was looking up at the trees.

"Well, Walter told me he likes Angus very much. He said Angus is a very nice boy."

Cassie smiled a little. "Yes. He is very nice."

"Is he your boyfriend?" Amelia asked.

"No! I don't have boyfriends!" shouted Cassie.

"Sorry." Amelia was embarrassed.

Cassie looked up at the trees. She rocked backwards and forwards. She sang to herself.

Well, I tried, thought Amelia.

Walter walked along the river, looking for Angus. Finally, he saw him. Angus was carrying a plastic bag. He was picking up garbage.

Walter waved to Angus, and walked towards him.

"Some people are pigs," said Angus. "Look at all this garbage they throw on the ground." He opened the bag and showed Walter the cans, bottles and fast food boxes he had picked up.

"Angus, I have to talk to you."

Angus looked away.

"I think you know why I am here," said Walter. "I think you know that Hatman had an accident."

"I don't know anything!" said Angus loudly. "But I heard they found an old man in the river. It can't be Hatman! He is my friend."

Walter took the photographs out of his pocket. He tried to give them to Angus, but Angus wouldn't take them.

"Angus! You have to help. I know it is difficult, but please tell me. Is one of these men, Hatman?"

He held up the photographs. Angus looked at them and looked away. "How would I know? Hatman always wore a hat and scarf."

"But you saw him without his hat and scarf, didn't you?"

"Once or twice." Angus wouldn't look at the photographs.

"Please, Angus."

Angus looked quickly at the photographs. His eyes filled with tears.

"One of these is Hatman, isn't it?"

"Yes. They are both Hatman." Angus rubbed the tears away from his face.

"Angus, I'm sorry. One of these men was found in the river."

"How did he die?"

"I don't know yet. I am waiting for the report. Then we will know and I will tell you."

Angus looked at Walter.

"Why would you tell me?"

"Because he was your friend," said Walter quietly.

Angus looked puzzled. "You said one of these men is Hatman. What do you mean?"

"There are two dead men. I know they look the same. One is Hatman, and the other is the man who died in the house across the road from the bus stop. The papers in his house say his name was Joseph Jones. It's a mystery and I need your help to solve it."

Amelia was tired of waiting for Walter. She tried to talk to Cassie again. "Who stays here with you, Cassie? Who are your friends?"

Cassie didn't look at her but she said, "Joey, Dolphin, Ruby and Angus. They are my friends."

"Do you know the old man who lives along the river?" Amelia asked Cassie.

Cassie sang and rocked, and wouldn't say any more.

Amelia saw Walter and a boy walking towards the camp.

"Who are you?" shouted Angus, running up to Amelia. He looked very angry.

Amelia stood up.

"I'm Amelia Bright. I work with Walter."

"Have you been talking to Cassie? Did you ask her questions? That is very bad!"

"Why is it bad? I only wanted to know if she had seen the old man." Amelia didn't understand why Angus was so angry.

Walter joined them. "Angus," said Walter. "What's wrong?"

"This woman has upset Cassie! Why is she here?"

"Amelia works with me. I tried to talk to Cassie, but she didn't want to talk to me. I asked Amelia to try. I thought maybe Cassie doesn't like men very much."

"That's true. She has very good reasons to be frightened of men. But no one should ask her questions. It makes her very unhappy. It will be a long time before she feels OK again."

"Oh, Angus. I'm sorry. I didn't know," said Walter. "I should have asked you first, but I couldn't find you."

"Please go away," said Angus.

"OK," said Walter. "Come on Amelia, we will go. And Angus..."

"What?"

"I'm sorry about Hatman, and I'm sorry we upset Cassie. But don't be angry with Amelia. It was not her fault."

12. MRS FRAMPTON CALLS THE POLICE STATION

Back at the police station, there was an email from Harriet. Walter opened the attached file. Amelia stood behind him and read it.

When Walter finished reading, he said, "That's very interesting. Bring a chair to my desk and we'll talk about it."

Amelia brought a chair and sat next to Walter.

Walter started talking. "Two men who look the same, die on the same night. One has a head cut that killed him. Harriet says the cut was caused by something heavy. Maybe a brick. She says there was nothing in the living room like that. The blood on the table came from the dead man but she thinks when he fell to the floor his head hit the table. But she doesn't think that caused the cut. So it was an attack. It was murder. The other man drowned. He had no food in his stomach but a lot of alcohol."

"So it wasn't murder," said Amelia.

"Maybe it was murder. Where did the whisky come from? If Hatman drank all the whisky and fell asleep, it would be easy to push him in the river. But I don't know."

"The men look the same," said Amelia. "But they are different too. Joseph Jones has soft hands. He had food, and his health was good. Hatman had bad teeth. Harriet said, 'It seems that for a long time he did not have enough to eat, and his hands were damaged. He worked hard with his hands. His fingernails are damaged, and he had many scars.'"

"I wonder," said Walter.

Just then, Walter's mobile phone rang. "Yes? Mrs Frampton. Can

I help you?"

Mrs Frampton talked for a while.

"Thank you. Yes, I think it is very important. I will come now."

Walter finished the call and stood up. "Mrs Frampton has remembered something. I'm going to see her now."

"What has she remembered?"

"There was another man in Skillington Road on Monday night and Tuesday. She didn't think it was important, but she has seen him again."

"I'll go with you," said Amelia.

"No. Stay here. Go through Harriet's report again. Make sure there is nothing else important there. I'll tell you all about Mrs Frampton's information when I come back."

13. WHAT MRS FRAMPTON SAW

Walter went to Mrs Frampton's house. He knocked, and Mrs Frampton shouted, "Come in."

As usual, she was sitting in her wheelchair looking out of the window.

Walter sat in an armchair. "So please, Mrs Frampton, what do you remember?"

"On Monday afternoon, there was a man standing outside my house. He was looking at the bus stop. I had never seen him before. He was a big man. He was wearing a baseball jacket and a baseball cap. I thought he was an American tourist, and I didn't think anything about it. Then I saw him on the street, on Tuesday morning. That was the day you found the old man's body. I saw him again today. He walked past my windows. I can't see the door to Joseph Jones' house, but I can see the path that goes to the door. He walked up it about an hour and a half ago. Then I saw him walk towards the side of the house."

"Thank you," said Walter. "And you are sure it is the same man?"

"I haven't seen his face, but the clothes are the same. I don't think he can be a tourist. Skillington Road is nice, but no tourist would come back here three times."

"I'm going next door now," said Walter. "Please lock your door. We don't know who this man is. I will come back after I look at the house."

Walter went to the front door of Joseph Jones' house. Everything was quiet. The door was locked. He walked around to the back of the house. The back door was open. Walter could see that the lock was broken.

Walter called the police station and spoke to Mary Jane. "I'm in Skillington Road. There has been a strange man around Joseph Jones' house for a few days. Someone has broken into the house. Can you send some uniformed police please?"

"Oh, Walter. I'm sorry. I can't. All the spare policemen are at a local bar. The other detectives think a big drug deal will happen. I'll call and ask them to send some policemen from there to Skillington Road, but I don't know when they will come."

"OK, I understand. I'll wait," said Walter.

As Walter was putting his phone back in his pocket, an arm came around his throat and someone pulled him into the house. He felt the man's other hand go into his pocket and pull out his phone. The man threw Walter's phone on the ground and jumped on it.

The man pushed Walter into a chair in the kitchen. Then the man tied him to the chair. The man tied rope around his arms and his legs. It was very tight. Walter saw the man's arms. He was wearing a baseball jacket. Walter could not see his face, but he was tall and strong.

The man didn't speak, but Walter could hear him breathing. He could smell him too. It was a strange smell – a mixture of meat and tobacco and something else, something sweet.

After a few minutes, Walter heard the man leave the kitchen. He was alone.

14. WHERE IS WALTER?

Amelia had read Harriet's report again and again. *The two dead men look the same,* she thought. *But the DNA results will come back on Monday.*

She sat at Walter's computer for a long time. It was almost 6:00pm when Mary Jane came into the detective's room.

"Did Walter call you?" she asked.

Amelia rubbed her eyes. She was tired. "No. He went to talk to Mrs Frampton, the woman who lives next door to Joseph Jones' house. She called. She said she had remembered something."

"Why didn't you go with him?"

"I wanted to. But Walter told me to stay here and read Harriet's report again."

"Walter called me. He said that a strange man had been seen around Joseph Jones' house. He said the lock on the back door was broken. He asked me to send some policemen. But I have no one to send. Walter said he would wait."

"What does Superintendent Pierce think?" asked Amelia.

"That man! He is an idiot! Sanjay called him, and said a big drug deal would happen at one of the local bars late this afternoon or tonight. Pierce called the TV station and drove down to the bar so he can be on TV! I called Superintendent Pierce and asked him to send some men to Joseph Jones' house, but he said the drug deal was more important, so Walter would have to wait."

"A drug deal is very important", said Amelia.

"If it is a drug deal," said Mary Jane, laughing. "I think someone stole some TVs and wants to sell them in the bar. You and Walter are looking at two murders. What is more important? And now there is no signal from Walter's phone. Maybe he turned his phone off, but I am worried."

Amelia jumped up. "I'll go."

"No," said Mary Jane. "You can't go alone."

"But I'm worried," said Amelia.

"I'm worried too. But I will not let you go alone. It might be dangerous. We will have to wait until Superintendent Pierce sends some uniformed policemen. Then you can go."

15. MRS FRAMPTON IS WORRIED

Mrs Frampton was worried. She looked through the window. It was a long time since Walter had gone to the house next door.

He said, 'I will come back', she thought. *If he found something, he would call for more policemen. But no police cars have come. His car is still parked outside my house. I think something is wrong.*

She picked up Walter's business card and called the number. There was no answer. Mrs Frampton thought it was very strange. *I have to do something. What can I do?*

She called the police station and talked to Mary Jane. Mary Jane said she would send some policemen as soon as possible. But 30 minutes later, no one had come.

Then she saw Angus walking along the road. She didn't know him, but her caregivers talked about him. They said he was a wonderful young person.

Mrs Frampton didn't stop to think. She picked up a heavy object from the table next to her chair. She threw it at the window. Mrs Frampton couldn't walk, but she had strong arms. The object broke the window. Angus heard the noise of breaking glass and looked at Mrs Frampton's house. Mrs Frampton waved and shouted. Angus came to the broken window to talk to her.

"I want you to do something for me," said Mrs Frampton.

16. ANGUS IN TROUBLE

Walter was very cold and uncomfortable. He had been tied up for hours. He could hear the mystery man moving around the house. It sounded like he was looking for something. Then he heard the sound of breaking glass. He heard loud bangs and crashes.

The man was coming down the stairs. He was pulling something heavy.

The man came into the kitchen. *Oh no!* thought Walter. The man was pulling Angus across the floor. Angus had blood all over his face, and his eyes were closed.

The man tied Angus' arms and legs. Then he kicked him in the back. "Stop that!" shouted Walter. "You could kill him!"

The man looked at Walter. He laughed. "I'm going to kill both of you. But it will be more convenient to make you walk down to the river when it is dark. After I kill you, I can push your bodies into the water."

He kicked Angus again. Then he went back up the stairs. *What is he looking for?* wondered Walter. *He speaks English well, but he is not English. Russian, maybe? I don't know.*

Walter watched Angus. He could not move to help him. After a little while, Angus made a noise.

"Angus! Can you hear me? Why are you here?"

Angus' voice was very quiet, and it seemed it was difficult for him to speak. "The woman next door, in the wheelchair. She was worried. She asked me to come and look for you. I saw the lock was broken. I saw a broken phone. I saw you tied to the chair. I climbed up to the second floor. I broke a window and climbed in, but that guy. He was waiting for me."

I hope help comes soon, thought Walter.

17. A TERRIBLE STORY

The man came back into the room and sat down at the kitchen table. He took his hat off. "Now we wait until it is very dark and the road is empty," he said.

He doesn't care that I can see his face. He is going to kill us, thought Walter.

"Uh. Did you find what you were looking for?" asked Walter.

"I found nothing. That is good. No papers, no letters, no diaries, no photographs. When I have killed you two, I will be safe."

"You killed the man who was living here. Who was he?"

"His name was Josip Horvat. He was a rat. I should have killed him in nineteen ninety two. He was a dirty Croat. I found him and I killed him. It makes me happy."

The man took a bottle out of his pocket and drank deeply. Walter thought it was some kind of alcohol, but it smelled like perfume.

"Are you Croatian?" asked Walter.

The man spat on the floor. "I am a true Serb. I am a hero. I hunted Bosniaks and Croatians. I worked for a pure Serbia."

"So the man who lived here came to England to hide from the Serbians?"

"No, no!" The man took another drink from his bottle. "He was hiding from other Croatians!

"In nineteen ninety two I was hunting Croatians and Bosnians in Prijedor in Bosnia. I found that rat, hiding in the back of a post office. I was going to send him to the prison camp at Omarska. But he said, 'If you let me go, I will tell you where about twenty Croatians are hiding'. And I said 'yes'.

"When we took those twenty Croatians to the prison camp, I told them about the man. He had told me their hiding place. Can you believe it? A few of them were young women, and one of them was his own brother! I have killed many people, but I do not believe in treating any woman badly and I believe in family."

Walter could see it was getting very dark outside. *I must keep him talking. Help must come soon!*

"So the brother didn't die in the prison camp? He was the man we found in the river?"

"You are right. The brother didn't die in the prison camp. I saw him at the bus stop. I knew who he was.

"It was easy. I gave him whisky. He talked and talked. When he got out of the prison, he looked for his brother. Their family had some cousins in England. He guessed his brother would come here. It took him many years, but he found him."

"But why didn't he talk to him? Why did he sit in the bus stop and look at his brother's house?" Walter didn't understand.

"I don't know. He was a crazy old man. Maybe he wanted his brother to feel bad. I guess his brother never knew who the old man in the hat was. After he drank all the whisky, he fell asleep. I pushed him into the river."

"Did you take the letters from the letterbox?" asked Walter.

"Yes. I found Josip Horvat because one of his old friends in Bosnia was writing to him. I thought there might be a letter to connect 'Joseph Jones' to 'Josep Horvat'. Then the police might find out about Omarska and me. It was lucky I took the letters. There was such a letter. I burnt them all.

"And now it is time for you and this young man to go to the river." He put his baseball cap on. He took a knife from the inside pocket of the baseball jacket and cut the ropes around Walter's arms and hands. He went to Angus. He put the knife against Angus' throat. "Undo the rope around your legs. You will walk to the river or I will kill him now."

"Just one thing," said Walter quickly. "I understand the story, but why did you kill the brothers?"

The man looked at Walter. "I am a hero, but the world says I am a war criminal. People are hunting me. I have been running and hiding for a long time. Josep Horvat, the rat, knew my face and knew my name. He knew what he had done, but he also knew what I had done. I want to stop running. I want a normal life. The only other person still alive who knew what I did, was the brother. It was a lucky thing when I found him here."

18. ELIZA

Eliza was bored. They had been at the bar for a very long time. She thought there was no drug deal. She thought Mark, Keith and Sanjay had made a big mistake.

She heard Keith talking to Mark. "It won't be long now. Then the new boss will know how good we are. Did you hear? That idiot, Walter, called and asked for policemen to go to Skillington Road. He said a strange man was in the area, and the lock to the old man's door was broken."

Mark laughed. "He can't be a real detective, so he says an accident is a murder. He wants everyone to think he is important. What did the new boss say?"

"The new boss is smart. He said this drug deal is more important. He said Walter must wait," said Keith.

"I hope he makes him wait all night," said Mark.

This is very bad, thought Eliza. *Nothing will happen here. And Walter might be in danger.*

Eliza tried to call Walter's phone. She got no answer. *Walter is fat and old fashioned,* she thought. *But, he knows the rules. He would never turn his phone off when he was on the job. Where is Amelia? Is she with him?*

"Mark," said Eliza. "Walter isn't answering his phone. Maybe something is wrong."

Mark and Keith laughed. "He doesn't know how to use a mobile phone. He's old and stupid. Don't worry about it."

He's not so old, and he is not stupid, thought Eliza. She called Amelia.

"This is Eliza. Where are you?"

"At the police station. Walter went out and didn't come back. Mary Jane says I cannot go out to look for him alone!" Amelia was very unhappy.

"OK," said Eliza. "I'm coming. Wait in the car park!"

Eliza ran to her car. She knew that she would be in trouble with Mark, Keith and Sanjay. She knew Superintendent Pierce would be angry, but she didn't care.

Amelia was standing in the car park. Eliza stopped the car and Amelia jumped in.

As Eliza drove quickly out of the police station she asked, "Did you talk to Mary Jane?"

"Yes. She said 'go, go, go'. She is very worried."

Eliza laughed. "I like Mary Jane."

Eliza drove fast. "When did Walter leave the police station?"

"Many hours ago," said Amelia. "The next-door neighbour, Mrs Frampton, called. Walter went to talk to her."

"I heard that Walter asked for some policemen to go to Skillington Road, but everyone was down at that bar. And Superintendent Pierce said Walter must wait," said Eliza.

Eliza drove into Skillington Road and slowed down. "That's Walter's car, isn't it?"

"Yes," said Amelia. "It's outside Mrs Frampton's house."

Eliza pulled into the side of the road about 100m away from Walter's car. "I don't know," she said quietly. "But I have a bad feeling. Let's walk from here."

The two women walked up to Mrs Frampton's house. The light was on in the front living room and the curtains were open. Amelia saw the broken window. She ran up and shouted to Mrs Frampton. "Who did this?"

"I did. I wanted to talk to that young boy - the one that lives down by the river. The other detective didn't come back, so I asked the boy to go and look for him. Now he hasn't come back either. Something is very wrong."

"Are you OK?" asked Eliza

"I've been sitting here looking at the road instead of watching TV, but I'm OK. If something has happened to that nice boy, I will never forgive myself."

"I promise we'll come back!" said Eliza. "But now Amelia and I are going next door."

"Be careful," said Mrs Frampton.

19. THROUGH THE WINDOW

Amelia and Eliza walked towards the next house. The front of the house looked quiet and normal.

They walked down the side of the house towards the back garden. Eliza stopped. "Wait," she said to Amelia. From the corner of the house they could see the back door was open. Eliza moved with her back against the wall of the house. She looked up. "There is a broken window upstairs," she said very quietly. "Stay here."

Eliza walked back towards the road and talked on her phone.

When she came back, she was very angry. "I called Mary Jane. I told her about Walter and the young boy. I told her about the open door and the broken window. Mary Jane said she has been calling Superintendent Pierce every ten minutes. He won't listen to her. He says he will not send extra policemen here. We will have to do this alone."

"What will we do?" asked Amelia. She was very frightened.

"We have to look inside the house. We must be very careful."

Amelia followed Eliza as she moved on her hands and knees along the ground to the back door. Eliza moved past the door and stopped. Amelia stopped next to the kitchen window with her back against the wall. She looked in.

She saw Walter standing next to a man in a baseball cap and jacket. The man had his arm around Angus' neck. In his other hand was a knife.

The man in the baseball cap was talking. Walter walked towards the door. The man followed carrying Angus. The man's arm was around Angus' neck. Angus' feet were above the ground.

Angus can't breathe. He'll die, thought Amelia.

She looked at Eliza, and put her finger to her mouth. *Don't say anything.*

Eliza nodded, *OK.*

Eliza saw Walter come out the door. She saw the man in the baseball cap and Angus hanging from his arm.

"Now!" shouted Eliza.

Eliza and Amelia jumped on the man in the baseball cap. He didn't see them, so he was very surprised. He dropped Angus. Walter pulled Angus away. Amelia and Eliza were lying on top of the man. He was big and strong and he was fighting. It was difficult for Amelia and Eliza to control him.

"Walter! Help!" shouted Eliza.

Walter left Angus lying on the ground. He came with a stone. He hit the man on the head. The man stopped moving. Eliza took handcuffs from her pocket and put them on the man.

She stood up and smiled at Walter. "Thank you! He was too strong for us."

Walter smiled too. "It was not good police work, but it worked."

"I like it!" said Eliza.

Walter and Amelia ran to Angus. "Is he OK?" asked Amelia.

"I think so. He must go to hospital, but I think he will be OK."

Eliza was shouting on her phone. "I don't care! We have a killer! We have a young boy who needs an ambulance. We have a detective who was attacked. Come now!"

An ambulance came and took Angus to the hospital. Superintendent Pierce came with the TV crew and reporters. The other detectives came too.

Superintendent Pierce walked up to Walter. "Tell me what to tell the media. What happened here? Was it important?"

Eliza opened her mouth. She wanted to shout at the Superintendent, but Walter signalled to her to be quiet.

"A war criminal was here in Wolling. He killed two people and tried to kill two more people. The Wolling Police have everything under control. The United Nations will be very interested. We will know more after we can discuss the situation with them," said Walter.

Superintendent Pierce smiled. He went back to the TV crew and the reporters. He said, "A war criminal came to Wolling. He killed two people and he tried to kill two more people. The Wolling Police have everything under control. The United Nations will be very interested. We will know more after we can discuss the situation with them."

20. THE NEXT DAY

Superintendent Pierce was very pleased. He was on the TV news. He was in the newspapers.

The man in the baseball cap was in prison. The international media were asking questions. Superintendent Pierce was a very happy man.

Walter went to the café near the second bridge. He was lucky. The kind woman who gave Angus the chocolate cake was working.

"Do you remember me?" asked Walter.

"Of course. You came here with Angus, and you bought him a milkshake. How can I help you?"

"Angus is in hospital. He is OK, but he was attacked when he was trying to help me," said Walter. "I am going to the hospital to visit him. But I hope you can help me. Why is Angus homeless?"

"Angus's mother was from Wolling, and his father was from the West Indies. They were in love. They were very happy. But his father didn't like living in England. Too wet. Too cold. He only stayed here because his wife didn't want to leave. Then Angus' mother died. Angus was maybe twelve years old. His father was broken-hearted. He went back to the West Indies. He left Angus with his wife's family. He thought Angus would have a better life here. But he was wrong. Angus' family didn't like having Angus in the house. They did not treat him well. Angus stayed with them for two years, and then he walked out, or maybe they told him to go. I don't know."

"It's a sad story," said Walter.

Walter went to the hospital. The doctor said Angus would be OK.

He could leave the hospital in one or two days.

Walter talked to Angus. "Why don't you come and live with me? You would have an address. You could study. It would be good for you."

"Thank you," said Angus. "But no. I don't want to live with you."

"OK. It's your choice. But take this card. It has my phone numbers and address on it. If you change your mind, you can come any time."

Walter's phone made a noise. He looked at his phone. It was a text from Mary Jane. Superintendent Pierce wanted Walter to go back to the police station.

"I have to go. But remember what I said."

As Walter was walking away from Angus' bed, he stopped. "Did you say 'no' because you don't want to leave the others?"

"Maybe."

Walter smiled. "I have eight bedrooms and three bathrooms. I live in a small hotel, but it is empty now. Only me. If you change your mind, you can all come."

"I don't think so," said Angus. "But thanks."

21. NOVEMBER

It was the coldest, wettest November than anyone could remember.

Walter wrote a letter of resignation. He said he wanted to retire. But Superintendent Pierce asked him to stay.

"He's smarter than I thought," said Mary Jane. "He was in the newspapers and on the TV when Walter, Amelia and Eliza caught that killer. He knows his best chance of looking good is to keep Walter here."

Amelia's sister found a new man. She took her children to live in his house. Amelia did not have to send her money anymore. Amelia and Eliza became good friends. They found an apartment together.

Sanjay, Mark and Keith didn't change at all. "Walter got lucky," they said. "He didn't know what he was doing. We do the real work around here. The boss is keeping him here because he feels sorry for him."

Amelia and Eliza looked at each other and laughed.

One night in the middle of November, Walter was sitting in his small living room watching TV. It was very windy. It was raining hard outside, and it was very cold.

He heard someone knocking at the back door. He went through the big kitchen and opened the door. It was hard to see anything, because it was so dark.

Walter turned on the outside light. He saw a row of shopping carts. He saw two young men with their arms around Cassie. She was wrapped in blankets. Then he saw Angus holding the hand of a young girl.

"This is Joey," said Angus, pointing to one of the young men. "And that's Dolphin."

"I'm Ruby," said the girl standing next to Angus.

"Cassie has asthma and she's going to have a baby," said Angus. "She can't stay down by the river. Can we stay here for a little while?"

Walter smiled and opened the door wider. "Come in! Come in!"

THANK YOU

Thank you for reading Pretty and Bright. (Word count: 14,760) We hope you enjoyed it.

If you would like to read more graded readers, please visit our website http://www.italkyoutalk.com

Other Level 3 graded readers include
A Dangerous Weekend
A Holiday to Remember
Akiko and Amy Part 1
Akiko and Amy Part 2
Akiko and Amy Part 3
Be My Valentine
Different Seas
Enjoy Your Business Trip
Enjoy Your Homestay
I Need a Friend
Old Jack's Ghost Stories from England (1)
Old Jack's Ghost Stories from England (2)
Old Jack's Ghost Stories from Ireland
Old Jack's Ghost Stories from Japan
Old Jack's Ghost Stories from Scotland
Old Jack's Ghost Stories from Wales
Party Time!
Stories for Christmas

The Curse
The Diary
Time to Go
Together Again
Who is Holly?

ABOUT THE AUTHOR

I Talk You Talk Press is an award-winning Japan-based publisher of language textbooks, graded readers and language learning/teaching resources.

Our team is made up of highly experienced language teachers and translators, who have all studied at least one additional language to an advanced level.

This experience enables us to design our materials from the perspective of both the teacher and the learner. We consult with both teachers and language learners when designing our textbooks and graded readers, and test our materials extensively in the classroom before publication.

We are a fast-growing press, and currently publish graded readers for learners of English. We publish new graded readers monthly.

www.ingramcontent.com/pod-product-compliance
Lightning Source LLC
Chambersburg PA
CBHW032216040426
42449CB00005B/616